Nov '87
To Stevie B:
Can't wait to see
you again. Cutie ♡
Love,
Aunt Mary
XXooo

WHEN FATHER PAPERED THE PARLOUR

Illustrated BY CAROLE TATE

M

Words and Music
R. P. Weston & F. J. Barnes

First published in 1981 by
MACMILLAN CHILDREN'S BOOKS
A division of Macmillan Publishers Limited
London and Basingstoke
Associated companies throughout the world

Our parlour wanted papering

Our parlour wanted papering, and Pa said it was waste
To call a paper-hanger in,

and so he made some paste.

He bought some rolls of paper, got a ladder and a brush,
And with my mummy's nightgown on at it he made a rush.

When Father papered the parlour,
  You couldn't see him for paste!
Dabbing it here, dabbing it there
– Paste and paper ev'rywhere.

Mother was stuck to the ceiling,
The children stuck to the floor,
I never knew a blooming family
So 'stuck up' before.

The pattern was 'blue roses' with its leaves red, white and brown;
He'd stuck it wrong way up and now, we all walk upside down.

And when he trimm'd the edging off the paper with the shears,
The cat got underneath it, and Dad cut off both his ears.

Soon Dad fell down the stairs
And dropp'd his paper-hanger's can
On little Henrietta sitting
There with her young man,

The paste stuck them together,
As we thought 'twould be for life,
We had to fetch the parson in
To make them man and wife.

We're never going to move away from that house any more,
For Father's gone and stuck the chairs and table to the floor,

We can't find our piano, though it's broad and rather tall,
We think that it's behind the paper Pa stuck on the wall.

Now, Father's sticking in the pub, through treading in the paste,
And all the fam'ly's so upset, they've all gone pasty faced.

While Pa says, now that Ma has spread the news from north to south,
He wishes he had dropped a blob of paste in Mother's mouth.

When Father papered the parlour, you couldn't see him for paste!
Dabbing it here, dabbing it there – Paste and paper ev'rywhere.
Mother was stuck to the ceiling, the children stuck to the floor,
I never knew a blooming family so 'stuck up' before.

Our parlour wanted papering

When Father Papered The Parlour

Written and Composed by

Tune Ukulele

WESTON and BARNES

Brightly, but not too fast

1. Our par - lour want - ed pa - per - ing, and
2. The pat - tern was 'blue ros - es' with its
3. Soon dad fell down the stairs and dropp'd his
4. We're nev - er going to move a - way from
5. Now, fath - er's stick - ing in the pub, through

pa said it was waste____ To call a pa - per - hang - er in, and
leaves red, white and brown;____ He'd stuck it wrong way up and now, we
pa - per - hang - er's can On lit - tle Hen - ri - et - ta sit - ting
that house an - y more,____ For fath - er's gone and stuck the chairs and
tread - ing in the paste,____ And all the fam' - ly's so up - set, they've

CHORUS

When 'fath - er pa - pered the par - lour, you could - n't see him for paste!____ Dab - bing it here, dab - bing it there Paste and pa - per ev - 'ry - where.